WORSHIP IS CELEBRATING AS LUTHERANS

by Walter M. Schoedel & David W. Christian

Publishing House
St. Louis

Copyright © 1990 by Concordia Publishing House
3558 S. Jefferson Ave., St. Louis, MO 63118-3968
Manufactured in the United States of America

Scripture quotations are from The Holy Bible: New International Version,
copyright © 1973, 1978, 1984 by the International Bible Society.
Used by permission of Zondervan Bible Publishers.

1 2 3 4 5 6 7 8 9 10 **AP** 99 98 97 96 95 94 93 92 91 90

CONTENTS

WORSHIP

WORSHIP IS . . .

1

— a word that is not easy to describe; we need to walk around it and view it from different perspectives. It takes more than just study and talk to understand worship. We need to experience worship and become immersed in it. Worship is something that must be done.

— a word that comes from an old English root meaning to show honor and worth.

— a word that translates a number of different Hebrew and Greek words from the Old and New Testaments. The Hebrew word most often used for worship means "to bow down." The Greek term for worship conveys two ideas: "showing reverence" and "practicing service."

— a noun which describes an encounter with God.

— a verb which expresses an active response in mind, emotions, will, and body to all that God is, says, and does for us in Jesus Christ.

— a drama. God himself has written the script and initiated the response of the participants. He has gathered us so that we might honor Him with our prayers, our proclamations of His word, and our praise of His name.

— a two-way interaction. Through it God becomes involved in the lives of the members of His church, so that we may be empowered to respond to Him.

— a holy conversation between God and His people. He speaks to us, and we in turn voice our prayers and praise.

WORSHIP IS . . .

To Us
Isaiah 43:1

IN LOVE
1 John 3:1; 4:10

GOD'S REACH

FROM HIS HEART
Isaiah 51:16

THROUGH JESUS CHRIST
In Word and Sacrament
1 John 2:1–2; 4:9

All worship begins with God. He created us and wants us to be with Him. He reaches out His hand to us, and, in worship, draws us ever more closely to Himself. Jesus, whom we come to know through Word and Sacrament, is the way God is revealed to us, and it is in His name that we approach the throne of the Almighty.

WORSHIP IS . . .

TO GOD
Psalm 95:6–7

THROUGH CHRIST
John 14:6

**TOGETHER WITH
FELLOW BELIEVERS**
Hebrews 10:25

THE BELIEVER'S REACH

IN THE MIND
Mark 12:30

FROM THE HEART
Psalm 130:1–2

WITH THE BODY
1 Corinthians 6:20

In worship the believer reaches out to his heavenly Father through Jesus Christ, who is the way to the Father. That reach goes on in his mind, as he is blessed with a consciousness of God as Creator, Redeemer, and Sanctifier. That reach comes from a heart that is aware of its need for God, and seeks fellowship with God in the company of fellow believers. That reach is expressed with the body as believers stand, sing, bow their heads, make the sign of the cross, and kneel at the altar.

WORSHIP IS . . .

The believer's response to God's love in Christ.

In worship, God **ACTS**. He

A bsolves the believer of his sins,

C onfirms the believer's faith in His promises,

T eaches the believer the way of life, and

S ends the believer His Spirit through Word and Sacrament.

In worship, the Christian **ACTS**. He

A dores God with a thankful heart,

C onfesses his sins and his faith,

T ells others the Good News, and

S erves God by serving others in His name.

WORSHIP IS . . .

CONFESSION

Confessing sins to God	1 John 1:8–9
Confessing sins to one another	James 5:16
Confessing faith in the living God	Romans 10:9–11
Confessing faith to people everywhere	Matthew 5:16

CONVERSATION

God speaking to people	John 8:47a
People speaking to God	Matthew 7:7–8
People speaking with one another	Romans 12:12–19

CELEBRATION

Glorifying God	1 Corinthians 6:20
Delighting in His presence	Zechariah 9:9
Serving God	Matthew 4:10

GROWING IN WORSHIP

1. What is worship? Discuss the following possible answers.
    * Worship is primarily my response to God.
    * Worship is God's people coming together to support, care, and strengthen one another.
    * Worship is not an option, but an essential part of being a Christian.
    * Worship is acknowledging God's supreme power and love.
    * Worship is an opportunity to experience communion with God and with others.
    * Worship involves our total being: mind, spirit, soul, and body.

2. Explain how each of the following people worshiped.

The Wise Men	Matthew 2:1–12
The Widow	Mark 12:41–44
The Angels	Luke 2:13
The Shepherds	Luke 2:15–20
Simeon	Luke 2:22–25
The Sick Man	John 5:1–15
The Early Christians	Acts 2:42–47
Paul	Acts 17:10–33

3. Explain what these verses say about worship:

Ephesians 5:19	John 4:23–24	Exodus 34:14
Psalm 55:14	Psalm 27:14	Philippians 2:10
Hosea 6:6	Revelation 5:13	Psalm 29:2

4. Study next Sunday's Old Testament, New Testament (Epistle) and Gospel readings, and write a summary of what they say about worship.

5. Write an "I believe" confession—a statement of faith that summarizes your beliefs about worship.

ORDER

W**O**RSHIP IS **O**RDER

2

Through the years, Christians have devised **Orders of Worship.** We call them **"liturgies,"** a Greek word which means **"public service, help, ministry."** We come to church not simply to be observers, but to serve God by listening, learning, speaking, singing, praying, praising, sharing, and keeping silent. The Lutheran liturgies are orders that Christians have used for centuries to respond to God's goodness, grace, and generosity.

In this chapter, we want to study the main service of the church, the Order of Holy Communion. We invite you to follow the text of this service by following Divine Service II, First Setting, as it appears on pages 158–77 in *Lutheran Worship.* Many parts of this order are the same or similar to orders used by other liturgical churches such as the Roman Catholic and Episcopal churches. Much of the order is drawn directly from the Bible. It was arranged and passed down to us by the early Christians.

The first step in learning the order is to review the **seven parts of worship**.

1. We prepare for worship. This is done through our meditations and Bible study at home and through our private meditations in the pew. While waiting for the service to begin, it is helpful to look at the hymns that will be sung, the lessons that will be read, and the prayers that will be used.

2. We confess our sins.

3. We reach out to God.

4. We think about God's Word.

5. We respond to His message.

6. We offer our gifts.

7. We commune at His table.

These parts are arranged into three sections: the **Service of Preparation**, the **Service of the Word**, and the **Service of the Sacrament**. Together, these three sections make up the whole worship order.

An Outline of
the Order of Holy Communion

The Service of Preparation

Parts of the Service

Explanation

The Prelude

Music helps draw us into an attitude of prayer and praise.

The Ringing of the Bells

This is the call to God's people "to enter the Lord's gates with thanksgiving and His courts with praise" (Psalm 100:4).

A Hymn of Invocation

We are a "singing church," so we follow the advice of the apostle Paul to teach and admonish "one another in psalms and hymns and spiritual songs, singing with grace in your hearts to the Lord" (Colossians 3:16). This hymn may be one of praise, prayer, or reflection on the season of the church year.

The Invocation

We call upon God to be present with us. We worship the triune God, remembering our Baptism in His name. **Amen** means **"So be it; it is true!"**

The Confession of Sins

We examine ourselves and publicly confess our sins. Such a confession at the beginning of the service provides a climate of acceptance. In spite of our sins, we are accepted by God, and in turn we can accept each other.

The Absolution or Declaration of Grace

Christ said to His disciples, "If you forgive anyone his sins, they are forgiven" (John 20:23). The pastor speaks for God and announces God's cleansing forgiveness to those who made confession.

The Service of the Word

From the time of the apostles down through today, an important part of the service has been the reading of the Scriptures, including the **Old Testament Lesson**, the **Epistle Lesson** from the New Testament, and the **Gospel Lesson**. The reason for including these readings is the Scriptural principle that God's Word is the only rule and guide for Christian faith and living. The Service of the Word concludes with the sermon (which is the preached word), the church's confession of faith in response to God's Word, and the prayers of God's people.

The Introit of the Day

Introit is a Latin word meaning "**he enters into.**" The Introit is a part of a psalm or hymn that announces the theme of the day and begins the Service of the Word. Many years ago the faithful would meet outside, then process into the church. The pastor and the people would chant psalms as they entered the sanctuary.

The Kyrie

Kyrie is a Greek word meaning "**O Lord.**" It is a cry to the Lord for help and strength. In ancient times, the crowds would shout "**Lord, have mercy**" as the king entered their town. The church has taken over this prayer to greet its King Jesus Christ in the church service. As the people long ago expected help from their king, so we Christians expect blessings from our Savior.

The Hymn of Praise

Two hymns of praise, *"Glory to God in the highest"* and *"This is the feast of victory,"* give the congregation the opportunity to praise God and express joy because Jesus is our victorious Savior. During Advent and Lent, the Hymn of Praise is omitted.

The Salutation

In the Salutation, the pastor and the congregation greet each other in the Lord's name.

The Collect of the Day

The main thoughts of the day are *collected,* or summarized, in this short prayer. The collects for the seasons of the church year have come to us from the rich treasury of the church's heritage.

9

The First Lesson

The first reading is from the Old Testament, except during the Easter season when it is from the Book of Acts. This reading usually relates to the Gospel for the day.

The Gradual

Gradual, a Latin expression meaning "**step**," is a Scripture passage for each season of the church year. It is a response to the First Lesson and a bridge to the Second Lesson. Sometimes a Psalm is sung or spoken.

The Second Lesson

The second reading is from one of the epistles (letters) in the New Testament.

The Verse

A verse from Holy Scripture is usually sung in preparation for the reading of the Gospel. There are general verses as well as specific verses for the seasons of the church year.

The Holy Gospel

The Gospel Lesson is a selection from the accounts of the life of our Lord recorded by the four evangelists, St. Matthew, St. Mark, St. Luke, and St. John. Because Christ is with us in the Gospel reading, we stand to honor his presence. We also sing versicles (short verses) before and after the reading of the Gospel. On certain festival days the minister may read the Gospel while standing among the people. He may be flanked by acolytes carrying candles who proclaim Jesus and His Word as the "Light of the world."

The Hymn of the Day

This hymn follows the theme of the readings and sets the stage for the sermon. Suggested hymns of the day are listed on page 976–78 of *Lutheran Worship*.

The Sermon

The pastor proclaims God's Word and applies that Word to modern life and problems. He stresses both what God demands of us (the Law) and what God does for us through Jesus Christ (the Gospel).

The Creed

After hearing the Word of God read and proclaimed, the worshiper responds with his confession of faith in the words of the **Nicene Creed**. It is customary for the Nicene Creed to be spoken when Holy Communion is celebrated and on major festivals. The **Apostles' Creed** is used at other times.

The Prayers

This prayer in the service follows the directive of the Apostle Paul to young Timothy, a pastor: "I urge, then, first of all, that requests, prayers, intercession and thanksgiving be made for everyone—for kings and all those in authority, that we may live peaceful and quiet lives in all godliness and holiness" (1 Timothy 2:1–2). For this reason, the hymnal says "prayers are included for the whole Church, the nations, those in need, the parish, and special concerns. The congregation may be invited to offer petitions and thanksgivings. The minister gives thanks for the faithful departed, especially for those who recently have died" (LW pages 168–69).

The Service of the Sacrament

The church has confessed its sins and been forgiven, and its faith has been nurtured through hearing the Word. The church now reaches the climax of the worship experience in the celebration of the Sacrament of Holy Communion. The following parts of the liturgy help the worshipers partake of the Holy Meal thoughtfully, thankfully, and joyfully.

The Offering

The gifts of God's people are a response to God's blessings "as God has prospered them" (1 Corinthians 16:2). Our offerings are for the support of the church. They enable the church to provide the written and spoken Word of God, Christian education and pastoral care, food, clothing, shelter, and a helping hand to those in need.

11

The Offertory

As the offerings are brought to the Lord's table, the worshipers sing the offertory to express gratitude for all of God's blessings, dedicate themselves to God, and request His continued blessings.

The Preface

Preface means "**introduction**." The pastor and people get ready to celebrate the Holy Meal by greeting each other and with an exhortation as to how to celebrate the Meal.

The Appropriate (or Proper) Preface

These words state why we should give thanks using words and ideas appropriate for the season of the church year.

The Sanctus

Sanctus is a Latin word meaning "**holy**." The Sanctus contains words from Isaiah's vision of God (Isaiah 6:3) and the crowd's response on Palm Sunday when Jesus entered the city of Jerusalem (Matthew 21:9). We join them in spirit by singing their words as we anticipate Christ's coming in the Sacrament.

The Lord's Prayer

We pray to God as our Father using the prayer of the family of God because the Lord's Supper is our family meal.

The Words of Institution

The pastor speaks the words which Jesus spoke when He instituted the Supper with His disciples in the Upper Room (Matthew 26:26–28, Mark 14:22–24, Luke 22:19–20, 1 Corinthians 11:23–26). With these words the bread and wine are consecrated, that is, set apart for God's use in this special meal.

The Peace

The greeting of peace which Jesus spoke on the first Easter is shared before we approach the altar to receive Him. In the Lord's Supper, the body and blood of Christ are truly present in, with, and under the bread and wine.

The Agnus Dei

Agnus Dei is a Latin phrase meaning "**Lamb of God**." John the Baptist spoke these words as he pointed to Jesus coming toward him (John 1:29). As Christ comes to us in the Holy Supper, we recognize Him as the Lamb of God sacrificed for us to free us from the bondage of sin and death.

The Administration of the Supper

As we kneel at the Lord's Table, the pastor invites us, "Take, eat; this is the true body of our Lord and Savior Jesus Christ, given into death for your sins. Take, drink; this is the true blood of our Lord and Savior Jesus Christ, shed for the forgiveness of your sins." After we receive the Sacrament we hear the comforting words spoken by the pastor, "The body and blood of our Lord strengthen and preserve you steadfast in the true faith to life everlasting." We respond, "Amen," for this is our sincere desire. It is a good practice to offer a silent prayer of thanks when we return to our pews. While the meal is being distributed, the congregation and/or the choir sing one or more hymns.

The Post-Communion Canticle

"Thank the Lord," "Lord, now You let Your servant go in peace," or an appropriate hymn is sung. The purpose is to offer our thanks and express our faith in what God has done for us and promises to do for us in the future.

The Prayer of Thanks

Once again we express our appreciation to our gracious God for giving us this Holy Meal through Jesus Christ, our Lord and Savior.

The Blessing

The blessing spoken by the pastor is the **Aaronic benediction**, the blessing God first gave to Aaron and the other priests to speak to the people of Israel (Numbers 6;23–27). Jesus Christ, our High Priest, has come to us in a special way through this Holy Meal. The blessing is God's promise that Christ will go with us as we leave the church and return to the world to serve Him. We sing "Amen" to affirm the blessing; "So be it—it is true!"

GROWING IN WORSHIP

1. During next week's celebration of the Lord's Supper, see how the hymns are related to the theme of the day.

2. When you attend the Lord's Supper, you are with Jesus Christ in God's presence in a most intimate way. Talk about what these other people did when they were with Jesus.
  a. The shepherds   Luke 2:8–20
  b. Simeon   Luke 2:25–35
  c. Anna   Luke 2:36–38
  d. Peter, James, and John   Matthew 17:1–9
  e. Isaiah   Isaiah 6:1–8
  f. A Crowd   Luke 19:28–38
  g. Zacchaeus   Luke 19:1–9

3. Discuss what it means when in worship
  • we offer the Lord our hearts;
  • we offer the Lord our hands;
  • we offer the Lord our prayers.

4. There are two kinds of activities in worship:
  a. Sacrificial—We offer to God the sacrifices of our prayers, praises, and gifts, all in response to His love for us. Sacrificial parts are done *for God* by the congregation or the pastor on behalf of the congregation.
  b. Sacramental—God gives to us His blessings through His Word which is read and proclaimed to us, and through His Sacraments, all out of His love for us in Jesus Christ. Sacramental parts are done *by God* or by the pastor on behalf of God for the benefit of the congregation.

  Take *Lutheran Worship* and turn to Divine Service II (page 158). Work through the service and decide which parts are sacrificial and which are sacramental.

5. Study the prayers in *Lutheran Worship* to be used before and after worship (page 127), and before and after receiving Holy Communion (page 128). Then write appropriate prayers in your own words.

6. Discuss the following:

- What are some other Scriptural ways to express the Trinity in the Invocation (for example, Creator, Redeemer, and Sanctifier)?

- The Kyrie is like "three cheers for the King."

- The Hymn of Praise, "This is the feast of victory," (Lutheran Worship, page 161) says that the worship service is like a feast. How is this true?

- Offerings could be "Thank You" notes instead of money.

- How can you keep your mind from wandering during the prayers?

- Is the Sanctus (pages 170–71) more like rock music or classical music?

- The Agnus Dei, sung right before the meal of Holy Communion (page 172), is like a table prayer. How is the prayer fulfilled during Holy Communion?

- How can you express your thanks to God after celebrating Holy Communion?

7. Write a collect for a certain day of the church year. For models, see the Collects of the Day listed on pages 10–123. Your collect should include

the addressee—a name of God;
a phrase describing God;
your petition or request;
the result in your life from God answering the prayer;
a doxology (formula of praise) to God in thanks.

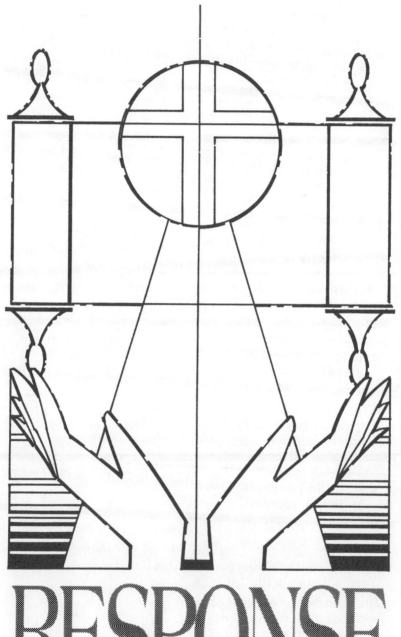

RESPONSE

WO**R**SHIP IS **R**ESPONSE

3

What do these statements from the introduction to *Lutheran Worship* suggest about who begins the worship act?

- Our Lord speaks and we listen.
- Saying back to Him what He has said to us, we repeat what is most true and sure.
- The rhythm of our worship is from Him to us, and then from us back to Him.

Whenever someone makes an aggressive movement toward us, we respond in some way. Very often we move away from the person. We may flinch, duck, or even run in the opposite direction. Through His Word and Sacraments, God makes a powerful move toward us. However, God does not intend to hurt or intimidate us, but to enfold us in His loving arms and make us a part of His family. He is the Prime Mover in our worship experience. Think through this statement from Martin Luther's explanation to the Third Article of the Apostles' Creed:

> I believe that I cannot by my own reason or strength believe in Jesus Christ, my Lord, or come to him; but the Holy Spirit . . . calls, gathers, enlightens, and sanctifies . . . (Luther's Small Catechism)

The apostle John put it this way: "We love because he first loved us" (1 John 4:19). Our worship is a response to God's gracious move toward us in Jesus Christ. Although our natural reaction might be to run away from God, hide from His presence, and ignore his call, he does not give up on us easily. Not only does He make the first move toward us, but He actually teaches us how to respond to Him. Through the Scriptures, He gives us the ideas and even the words to speak back to Him. Our liturgy, developed over the centuries, gives us a way of organizing our encounter with God, and it serves as a medium through which we express our membership in God's Kingdom and our faith and commitment to Jesus Christ.

Our response to God is much more than just "going to church." We are the church, and our worship pattern reflects our active response to His grace. Think of the many things that we do in a worship service. We stand, sit, kneel, speak, sing, and offer gifts. (Can you think of other things we do?) One way to organize all these different practices is to think of ourselves as involved in the following **ACT**ivities:

A CTS OF DORATION

We honor God by telling Him what He means to us, how much we love Him, and how wonderful He is.

Examples of adoration in the Bible include Exodus 15:1–2; 1 Chronicles 29:10–11; 2 Chronicles 2: 14–15; Nehemiah 9:6; Romans 11:33–36; Ephesians 3:20–21; and Philippians 2:10–11.

A C TS OF ONFESSION

We speak to God of our sins, and we say to Him and to each other what we believe about Him.

Biblical confessions of sin include Psalm 32; Psalm 51; and 2 Samuel 11:13; Biblical confessions of faith include Mark 8:27–29; Luke 7:1–10; John 20:24–31; and Romans 10:9–11.

AC**T**S OF
HANKSGIVING
Through words and songs, offerings and personal devotions, we
say "thank You" to God for His involvement in all areas of our lives.

Biblical models of thanksgiving include 1 Chronicles 29:12–13; Job 1:21; Psalm 34:1; Psalm 136; Ephesians 5:20; and Colossians 3:16.

ACT**S** OF
UPPLICATION
We pray for our own needs, the
needs and welfare of others, the
church, our communities, and the
world.

Biblical exhortations to pray include Psalm 34:4; Psalm 50:15; Colossians 1:9; 1 Thessalonians 5:17; James 5:13–14; and 1 Timothy 2:8.

Here is another way to think of the activities of worship:

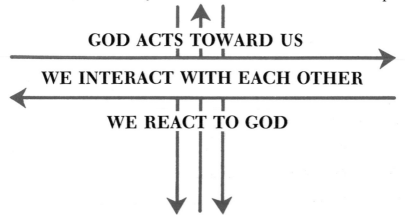

GOD ACTS TOWARD US

WE INTERACT WITH EACH OTHER

WE REACT TO GOD

Notice the "shape" of this response. Discuss the relation-ship between this shape and the central reason for Christian worship.

Indicate which of the three movements seems to be predominant in each part of the Divine Service listed below. Some parts may have all three movements, but usually one of the movements is most important for that part.

	God's action toward us	Our reaction to God	Our interaction with each other
HYMN			
INVOCATION			
CONFESSION			
ABSOLUTION			
KYRIE			
HYMN OF PRAISE			
SALUTATION			
READING OF SCRIPTURE			
SERMON			
CREED			
PRAYER OF THE CHURCH			
OFFERING			
SANCTUS			
SHARING THE PEACE			
AGNUS DEI			
HOLY COMMUNION			
THANK THE LORD			
BENEDICTION			

Worship the Lord

Fred Kaan

Ron Klusmeier

Refrain

Wor-ship the Lord, _____ (Wor-ship the Lord,) ___
Wor-ship the Fa - ther, the Spir - it, the Son, ___
Rais-ing our hands _____ (Rais-ing our hands) ___ in de -
vo-tion to him ___ who is One. _____

Stanzas

1. Rais-ing our hands as a sign of re - joic - ing _____
And with our lips our to - geth - er - ness voic - ing, _____
Giv-ing our-selves ___ to a life of cre - a - tive-ness.
Wor-ship and work ___ must be one! _____ *Refrain*

(continued on page 22)

(continued from page 21)

2. Praying and training that we be a blessing
   And by our workmanship daily expressing
   We are committed to serving humanity.
   Worship and work must be one.
   Refrain.

3. Called to be partners with God in creation,
   Honoring Christ as the Lord of the nation,
   We must be ready for risk and for sacrifice.
   Worship and work must be one.
   Refrain.

4. Bringing the bread and the wine to the table,
   Asking that we may be led and enabled,
   Truly united to build new communities.
   Worship and work must be one.
   Refrain.

5. Now in response to the life you are giving,
   Help us, O Father, to offer our living,
   Seeking a just and a healing society.
   Worship and work must be one.
   Refrain.

Naturally, our response to God's grace goes beyond the time and space of a Sunday morning experience. Some churches have signs at the entrance and exit that say:

ENTER TO WORSHIP
EXIT TO SERVE

There is a close connection between our corporate worship and our daily work. A Christian's response to God's love flows out of the doors of His church and into the world. Discuss and sing the powerful song on page 21. What new insights does it give you about worship?

GROWING IN WORSHIP

1. Look in a concordance under the word *altar*. In the Old Testament, which people built altars? Why did they build them? Develop a presentation around the responses of people who built altars to the Lord.

2. Find a hymn that is an example of each of the three movements in worship.

   God Acts — Hymn _____
   We React — Hymn _____
   We Interact — Hymn _____

3. Find out what opportunities your church provides in addition to the regular worship services for you to respond to God's love. Is there a board or committee for evangelism? for social ministry? for community service? Visit the meeting or talk to the head of the committee. You may wish to become involved in one of the projects.

4. Our response to God involves our whole being. All five senses are employed in the act of worship. Make a list of when each sense is used:

5. Discuss why we use our bodies the way we do in worship, including standing, kneeling, bowing our heads, making the sign of the cross, etc.

SYMBOL

WOR**S**HIP IS **S**YMBOL

4

Jesus used symbols when he walked the roads of Palestine. He referred to himself as the Good Shepherd, the Door, the Vine, and the Light of the World. When He taught His disciples, He spoke in parables, which are rich in symbolism.

We use symbols in our everyday activities. When we shake hands, that is a symbol of friendship. When we write a check, that represents money in the bank which we are spending. When we hear a siren, that signifies trouble.

Down through the centuries, God's people have used symbols to express their faith. One can hardly visit a church or pick up a Christian book or magazine without seeing a Christian symbol. Such symbols help communicate the Gospel, nurture our faith, and create an atmosphere that helps us worship. They serve as "road signs" for our earthly pilgrimage.

There are many Christian symbols. Some of them are well known, but many Christians do not know the message that the symbol originally was designed to communicate. In this chapter we will explain some of the most common symbols.

By using symbols and knowing what they stand for, the worshiper can have a deeper appreciation of the Gospel message and greater involvement in the worship experience. Symbols are useful tools for the private devotions of Christians and their instruction in the Christian faith. They are action signs for a person's spiritual journey.

THE HOLY BLESSED TRINITY

In the Athanasian Creed we confess "And the catholic [universal Christian] faith is this, that we worship one God in three persons and three persons in one God . . . the Unity in Trinity and the Trinity in Unity is to be worshiped" (*Lutheran Worship* pages 134–35). We hear God in the Scriptures speaking of Himself as being three persons (Father, Son, and Holy Spirit), but the three persons are only one God. That is why we refer to Him as the Trinity, which means "three in one."

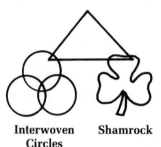

Interwoven Circles   **Shamrock**

The **triangle** has served as the common symbol for the Trinity. Each equal side represents a person of the Godhead. Together the sides form one complete Being.

The **shield** is found in many different forms, yet the message of each is the same: the Father is God, the Son is God, and the Holy Spirit is God. The distinct character of each person is indicated by the words "is not."

To communicate the concept of the Trinity, the church's symbols have also included the designs of three equal arcs, three interwoven circles, and a flower like a shamrock. Tradition tells the story of how St. Patrick saw a **shamrock**, a yellow flower with three leaves. He picked it and said, "God is like this flower; this flower has three petals, and the three petals form this shamrock. So God consists of three persons, and yet He is one God."

GOD THE FATHER

The hand, appearing in various forms, is the most common symbol of God the Father. The Old Testament speaks frequently of the hand of God, e.g., "my times, O Lord, are in Your hands" (Psalm 31:15). The hand signifies power, protection, and possession, as the Israelites sang after God saved them from the Egyptian army: "Your right hand, O Lord, was majestic in power. Your right hand, O Lord, shattered the enemy" (Exodus 15:6).

The **hand** of God is seen emerging from a cloud reaching down to bless His people. The hand of God with a circle depicts God as being eternal with an eternal concern for His people.

The **eye** is another common symbol for God the Father. It conveys the message that He sees us. "But the eyes of the Lord are on those who fear Him, on those whose hope is in His unfailing love" (Psalm 33:18).

The **Eye of God** signifies God's loving care and concern for His creation. It also reminds us that God sees everything we do. Jesus reminds us that God notices our faithful Christian actions even when no one else does: "pray to your Father, who is unseen. Then your Father, who sees what is done in secret, will reward you" (Matthew 6:6).

GOD THE SON

There are many symbols to represent God the Son, Jesus Christ, our Lord and Savior. There are monograms representing His name, crosses representing His crucifixion, and pictures depicting events during His ministry.

The Monograms

A **monogram** is usually two or more letters, such as initials, that identify a person. The early Christians made use of monograms to acknowledge that they belonged to Jesus.

IHS are the first two letters and the last letter of the Greek name for Jesus written in Greek capital letters, **IHSOYS. Jesus** means "**the Lord saves**." The monogram IHS is often written on altars and paraments.

Chi Rho (pronounced key row) are the first two letters of the Greek word for Christ, **Xristos. Christ** means "**Anointed One**." Old Testament prophets and kings were anointed— olive oil was poured on their heads— to consecrate them to God. Christ was consecrated for His ministry at His baptism.

Alpha and Omega are the first and last letters of the Greek alphabet. Jesus said, "I am the Alpha and the Omega, the First and the Last, the Beginning and the End" (Revelation 22:13; see also Revelation 1:8; 21:6). Jesus is the beginning and the end of all things; the world was created through Him (John 1:3) and one day He will come again to bring this world to a close (Revelation 22:12).

THE CROSS

More than **four hundred various shapes** of the cross have been used by Christians down through the centuries. Some of them have become identified with a particular community of Christians. The cross reminds us of the words of the apostle Paul, "We preach Christ crucified" (1 Corinthians 1:23). The Romans used many different types of crosses for crucifying, and we simply do not know exactly which type was used to crucify Jesus Christ because the Bible does not describe it in detail.

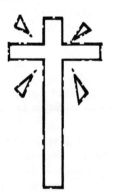

The **Latin Cross** is the most common form of cross. There are many variations of this design.

The **Jerusalem Cross** represents the five wounds of our Lord in His hands, feet, and side from the spear. The four small crosses may also indicate the four corners of the earth to which the message of the cross is to be proclaimed.

The **Celtic Cross** with a circle around the middle signifies that the message of the cross is eternal.

THE PICTURES

Jesus referred to Himself as the Vine, the Bread, the Door, and as other symbols. Christian artists down through the centuries have drawn pictures to communicate the message of Jesus Christ.

The **butterfly** is a symbol of Christ's resurrection and of eternal life for believers.

The **phoenix** rising from flames is another symbol of Christ's resurrection. A nonbiblical Greek legend says that the phoenix, an imaginary bird, lived several hundred years in a row before dying. The bird was then burned up, but would rise again from its own ashes and live several more hundred years before repeating its death and "resurrection." Christians borrowed this pagan myth and applied it to Christ.

The **lamb** illustrates Jesus as "the Lamb of God who takes away the sin of the world" (John 1:29). Sometimes the Lamb of God is pierced with His blood flowing into a chalice, showing that He gives us His blood, shed for us for the forgiveness of sin, in the Lord's Supper.

GOD THE HOLY SPIRIT

In contrast to the large number of symbols for Jesus Christ, there are few for God the Holy Spirit. There are fewer direct references in the Bible to the Spirit than to the Father and the Son, and it is harder to picture the Spirit because the Spirit usually is not described in physical terms. The words of Christ indicate the difficulty of "pinning down" the Spirit through a symbol: "The wind blows wherever it pleases. You hear its sound, but you cannot tell where it comes from or where it is going. So it is with everyone born of the Spirit" (John 3:8; in both Hebrew and Greek, the same word can mean either "wind" or "Spirit").

The **descending dove** is the most common symbol of the Holy Spirit. In creation, the Spirit hovered over the waters (Genesis 1:2; the same Hebrew verb is used of a bird hovering in Deuteronomy 32:11). At the baptism of Jesus, the Spirit descended bodily in the form of a dove (Luke 3:22).

The **seven-fold flame** commemorates the coming of the Holy Spirit in the form of tongues of fire on Pentecost (Acts 2:1–4). In the Bible (particularly in Revelation), the number seven often represents the holiness and perfection of God. The one Holy Spirit is often described as seven-fold (Revelation 4:5; 5:6) and as **bestowing seven gifts or fruits** (cf. Revelation 5:12).

THE FOUR EVANGELISTS

The writers of the four Gospels are called evangelists because they proclaim the good news of Jesus Christ. Symbols for the four Gospel writers have existed ever since the early days of the church. The artists were influenced by the vision of the prophet Ezekiel who saw four creatures supporting the throne of God. "Their faces looked like this: Each of the four had the face of a man, and on the right side each had the face of a lion, and on the left the face of an ox; each also had the face of an eagle" (Ezekiel 1:10). John saw a similar vision of four creatures resembling a man, a lion, an ox, and an eagle (Revelation 4:7).

The **winged man** represents St. Matthew because his gospel emphasizes the manhood or humanity of Christ. It begins by listing the human ancestors of Jesus.

The **winged lion** represents St. Mark because his gospel emphasizes the power and miracles of Christ.

The **winged ox** represents St. Luke because his gospel emphasizes the sacrificial death of Christ, and oxen were often used as sacrificial animals.

The **winged eagle** represents St. John because his gospel emphasizes the deity of Christ. The eagle soars higher than any other animal up toward heaven.

Tradition tells us that these four symbols represent major events in Christ's life: the winged man, His incarnation; the winged ox, His death; the winged lion, His resurrection; and the eagle, His ascension.

THE HOLY APOSTLES

Most of the symbols of the apostles depict the main characteristic and the manner of death of the apostle they represent. The symbols for Peter and Philip have a Biblical basis. The symbols for the other apostles are based on church tradition, and the stories behind the symbols are probably true.

St. Peter
After Peter's confession of faith, Jesus said that he would give him the keys to the kingdom of heaven (Matthew 16:16–19).

St. Andrew
According to church tradition, St. Andrew was martyred on a cross shaped like an X.

St. James the Elder
The three scallops are symbols of his long pilgrimage. Other symbols of traveling are also used for him, such as the staff and hat. Herod Agrippa had him killed with a sword (Acts 12:2).

St. John
Tradition holds that an attempt was made to kill John by giving him a chalice with poison in it, but he did not die.

St. Philip
The two loaves of bread signify Philip's involvement in the Feeding of the Five Thousand (John 6:7). The cross signifies that, according to tradition, Philip was crucified.

St. Matthew
The three purses symbolize that Matthew was a tax collector before Jesus called him to be an apostle (Matthew 9:9).

St. James the Lesser
Tradition says that St. James was martyred and sawed into pieces.

St. Jude
Judas son of James (Luke 6:16) was also called Thaddaeus (Matthew 10:3). He is said to have traveled by ship on his missionary journeys together with St. Simon.

St. Thomas
The carpenter's square represents the tradition that he built a church in India with his own hands. It is believed that he was martyred with a spear.

St. Bartholomew
The Bible represents his great faith in the Word of God, and the knife represents the tradition that he was skinned alive.

St. Simon	Also called Zelotes, his symbol means that he became a great fisher of men through the power of the Word of God.
Judas	Judas, who betrayed Christ, has only the darkness and emptiness of hell.

THE MEANS OF GRACE

To bring the Gospel message of love and forgiveness into our lives, God has given us His Holy Word and His blessed Sacraments, Baptism and the Lord's Supper. Because God conveys His grace to us through the Word and Sacraments we speak of them as the means of grace. There are many symbols depicting the use and message of the means of grace.

The **lamp** is a reminder of the words of the psalmist, "Your word is a lamp to my feet and a light for my path" (Psalm 119:105). The open Bible indicates that the Bible is to be read. "[They] examined the Scriptures every day" (Acts 17:11).

The **shell** with three drops of water reminds us of baptism when water was poured on us three times in the name of the Father and of the Son and of the Holy Spirit.

The **chalice** is a reminder of the cup which our Lord blessed at the Last Supper and which we share in the Lord's Supper.

THE CHURCH

The church is the body of believers in Christ who have been called by God in their baptism to be His very own and are nurtured in the faith through the Word of God and the Lord's Supper. Through the Holy Spirit, each member receives gifts for building the church. Through the years numerous symbols for the church have been developed. The following are most familiar:

The **vine and branches** recall the words of Jesus, "I am the vine; you are the branches" (John 15:5). This speaks of the church's dependence on Christ for her life and growth.

The **ark with the rainbow** reminds us of God's covenant with Noah (Genesis 9:13) and the new covenant He made with us in Jesus Christ (Luke 22:20).

The **cross and orb** represent the mission of the church to proclaim the gospel throughout the world. This design also depicts the triumph of the gospel over the world.

The **ship** depicts the church carrying the faithful safely across the stormy seas of life.

The **cross on the mast** symbolizes the message of Jesus Christ which empowers and guides the church. The term for the part of the church where the congregation sits, the nave, means "ship."

STARS AND CANDLES

Lights, particularly oil lamps and candles, have been used for both practical and symbolic purposes in the church from the earliest times. Today candles are still used in the church because of their symbolism. They stand for Christ who is the Light of the world.

Stars with different numbers of points have always had symbolical meanings.

The **six-pointed star** is the **Creator's star,** a symbol of creation because God completed His work in six days.

The **five-pointed star** is known as the **Bethlehem star,** and reminds us of the Wise Men to whom God revealed the Christ (Matthew 2:1–11).

The **two candles** on the altar emphasize the two natures of Christ, divine and human.

The **seven candles** in the candelabras beside the altar symbolize the seven gifts of the Holy Spirit (Revelation 5:12) and the seven churches (Revelation 1:20).

ADDITIONAL SYMBOLS

The fish is one of the oldest symbols for Christ. The Greek word for fish is "IXThYS." The **I** stands for **Iesous,** Jesus; the **X** stands for **Xristos,** Christ; the **Th** (one letter in Greek) stands for **Theou,** or God; the **Y** stands for **Yios,** Son; and the **S** stands for **Soter,** Savior. Therefore, the fish stands for "Jesus Christ, Son of God, Savior."

An **angel** is always associated with a message from God, such as the birth of Christ which the angels announced to the shepherds on the first Christmas Eve (Luke 2:8–20).

The **rose** can represent Jesus Christ (cf. Song of Solomon 2:1). It can also serve as a reminder of Isaiah's prophecy that the desert shall blossom as a rose at the coming of the glory of God (Isaiah 35:1).

Crowns can represent the Wise Men, the kingdom of God, and the suffering of Christ on the cross.

A **lily** can be a symbol of purity, and of the Virgin Mary in particular. However, it is used most often at Easter time as a symbol of resurrection. The lily bulb looks lifeless but it produces a beautiful flower, symbolizing life emerging from death.

 **Luther's Coat of Arms** is a cross within a heart, resting on a rose representing Christ, surrounded by a gold circle. Luther himself described its meaning as follows: The cross in the heart signifies that faith in Christ crucified within our heart saves us. The heart is on a white rose to show that faith gives peace and joy. The rose is on a sky-blue background to show that our joy now is a small taste of the future joy of heaven. The gold circle indicates that joy in heaven is endless and more precious than gold. There is a poem on the reverse side: "The Christian's heart is resting on roses, Even while beneath the cross it reposes."

A **scroll** reminds us of the many writings of the prophets, apostles, and the evangelists. Many parts of the Bible were originally written on scrolls (Jeremiah 36).

A **sheaf** of wheat can be used to depict God's blessings, a spiritual harvest, or the bread used in the Lord's Supper.

Trumpets in the Bible are used to call people to worship and to announce glorious messages, the Day of Judgement, and the resurrection.

Torches signify witnessing for Christ. As Christ said, "Let your light shine before men, that they may see your good deeds and praise your Father in heaven" (Matthew 5:16).

GROWING IN WORSHIP

1. Look around your church at the altar, the paraments, and any stained-glass windows. What symbols do you have in your church? Why are they located where they are? Ask the pastor to show your class his stoles and explain the symbols on them. The next time you worship in church, notice all of the symbols and think about what they mean.

2. Look in a concordance for the many passages in the Old Testament which speak of the hand of God. What do they say to you about God the Father?

3. Decide what crosses may best represent the following seasons of the church year: Advent, Lent, Epiphany, and Easter.

TAU CROSS   CROSS OF GLORY   LOOPED CROSS

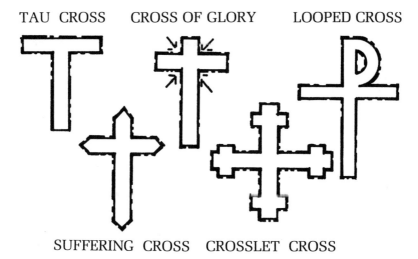

SUFFERING CROSS   CROSSLET CROSS

4. Create a symbol of your own, your own Christian coat of arms like Luther had, that depicts your faith.

WORS**H**IP IS **H**ALLELUJAH **5**

Language is perhaps the most important element of any relationship. People find out about each other by talking and listening. We initially make decisions about our relationships with others based on our conversations with them. We continue and deepen those relationships by various forms of communication. We talk together—in person, over the phone, and in letters or cards—to maintain our relationship. When we have an argument, when our feelings are hurt, or when a misunderstanding occurs, we must talk to each other to repair the damage to our friendship, and new levels of understanding and care are reached as we communicate on deeper and deeper levels.

Communication is also an important part of our relationship with God. From the beginning of time, the people of God have used language to express and celebrate their relationship with Him. Our worship is a process of voicing in external words and phrases our inner experience with God. The language of our worship, then, is extremely important. What is true of our relationships with others is even more true of our relationship with God. In worship that relationship is
    established,
            maintained,
                    repaired, and
                            transformed.

A crowd at a ball game gathers to cheer the mighty works of their team. They are there to honor the players, to praise their good qualities, to get the players' autographs, and to learn about their favorite players as they watch them in action. We hear special cheers that honor the team and describe certain actions of the game. There seems to be a special "ritual language" that surrounds sporting events.

In an even more real and important sense, we are gathered by the Holy Spirit to "cheer" the mighty acts of God. We received his "autograph" in our baptism; we have studied the "players"—God the Father, God the Son, and God the Holy Spirit—so we can be even more involved with them as the action of worship takes place. There are special words and phrases that identify us as the people of God. One example is the word

Hallelujah!

Hallelujah means "**praise the Lord**," and you hear it used most frequently in gatherings of God's family. It is a special "church cheer," and its regular use as a part of our liturgical action helps us put into words our relationship with God. There are other phrases, such as the Salutation ("the Lord be with you . . . ") and the Peace ("the peace of the Lord be with you always") which give shape and substance to our conversation when we gather together for worship.

Remember: we don't just "go to church" or "attend church"; **we *are* the church**. Our use of worship language need not be limited to the hours we spend in the church building. Much of what we have to say about God—the content of our personal witness—comes from the language that we use in our weekly worship:

- We live out our baptism through daily repentance and forgiveness (the **Invocation**).
- We work for peace, justice, and mercy in our families and in our neighborhoods (the **Peace**).
- We greet each other as brothers and sisters in Christ (the **Salutation**).

The language of our worship sets the pattern for our daily living and helps us to witness to the love and lordship of Jesus in our everyday lives.

Page through the liturgy that you use on Sunday and identify words or phrases that you can actually use in your day-to-day conversations outside church. Practice using this language with your class and with your family at home.

We have said it before: God speaks and we listen. Saying back to Him what He has already said to us in the Bible, we repeat what is most true and sure. In the Bible, God not only tells us about Himself, but also gives us the language we need to respond to Him in worship.

The five songs of the "ordinary" part of the Divine Service (more about the words *proper* and *ordinary* in the next chapter) are good examples of how God has equipped us through the stories of Scripture with language that shapes our worship response. These five songs are normally sung (or spoken) whenever we use the complete communion liturgy. Drawn from the stories of Scripture, these songs provide us with a comprehensive outline for corporate worship, as well as a body of substantial and significant language for our daily Christian experience and our private prayers. Let's take a brief look at each of them.

THE KYRIE
("Lord, have mercy . . .")

In the Kyrie we ask God for those things that only He can give. As we pray the Kyrie, we recognize our dependence upon God for the greatest gift of all—the forgiveness of sins (see the story of the Pharisee and the Tax Collector, Luke 18:10–14). We also exercise our privilege as His children to bring before our Father in heaven all our needs (see the story of Blind Bartimaeus, Mark 10:46–52).

How should we sing this song in church—quickly or slowly, loudly or softly, standing or kneeling? How can you use the language of the Kyrie in your personal prayers?

The Hymn of Praise
("Glory to God in the highest . . . ")

A host of angels sang this song at the birth of Jesus (Luke 2:13–14; the Lamb of God theme is from John 1:29). This was not a cute choir in pretty robes, but an army of heaven's best, gathered to do battle against the forces of Satan who would do everything in their power to thwart God's plan for our Savior to be born, live, die on the cross, and rise again. The angels announce to the whole universe God's salvation in Christ which brings "glory to God in the highest and peace to his people on earth."

When we sing the hymn of praise, we join the ranks of the angels in heaven and the militant Christian church on earth, lining up behind Jesus to go into battle against the powers of hell itself. One of the best ways to rout the devil and his legions is to sing praises to God and proclaim Jesus Christ, the Lamb of God who takes away the sin of the world, who now is seated at the right hand of the Father in power.

The alternate Hymn of Praise, "This is the feast of victory," also stresses the battle theme. It is based on Revelation 5:6–13. Jesus Christ is the Lamb who was slain, but He has won the victory over sin, death, and the devil, and now He reigns in power, wisdom, strength, and glory. All creation responds by singing His praises.

Could you improve the singing of the Hymn of Praise in your congregation?

How can you use the language of the Hymn of Praise in your personal prayers?

The Creed
("I believe in God . . . ")

Throughout the Scriptures, we read of people who confessed their faith. Indeed, the whole Bible is a confession, inspired by the Holy Spirit, of what the writers believe to be true about God. Look at

* the actions of Noah (Genesis 6–8);

- the Song of Moses (Exodus 15);
- the prayers of David (1 Chronicles 17, 29) and Solomon (2 Chronicles 6);
- the words of Job (Job 19:25);
- the confession of Peter (Luke 9:20) and his sermon on the Day of Pentecost (Acts 2); and
- the cry of the thief on the cross (Luke 23:36–43).

How often do we say "I believe" in our worship services? Why should you eagerly anticipate the opportunity to make this statement?

How can you use "creedal" language (I believe . . .) in your personal prayers?

THE SANCTUS
("Holy, holy, holy Lord . . .")

This song is a high point of the liturgy. God gave both the prophet Isaiah (Isaiah 6) and the apostle John (Revelation 4) glimpses of His heavenly glory. Both visions were accompanied by a mighty song of praise that extolled the holiness and majesty of God. As we approach the table of the Lord to receive Holy Communion, we, too, join the "angels, archangels, and all the company of heaven" to proclaim the majesty and mystery of God's salvation and to praise the name of Jesus Christ, the one who "comes in the name of the Lord" (Matthew 21:9).

Think of some ways to make this song an even more exciting event in the liturgical action.

How can you use this language in your personal prayers?

THE AGNUS DEI
("Lamb of God . . .")

With these words, John the Baptist identified Jesus as the fulfillment of all the expectations of the Old Testament believers and the hope of all who trust in the mercy of our gracious God (John 1:29). The song reminds us that the forgiveness of sins, God's free gift to us, was bought at the price of the death of His Son. We conclude these five songs as we begin them, with a request for God's mercy and peace.

Is this song best sung or spoken? Should it be done loudly or softly?

How can you use this language in your personal prayers?

THE RICHNESS OF POETIC EXPRESSION

The most memorable and meaningful lines of the liturgy portray vivid images for us. Read carefully the following passages and describe or sketch what you see in your imagination as you read the words.

- The Confession and Absolution (page 158)
- The End of the Preface: "Therefore with angels and archangels and with all the company of heaven we laud and magnify your glorious name, evermore praising you and saying . . . "
- The Words of Institution (page 171)
- The Lord's Prayer (page 171)
- The Benediction (page 174)

THE HYMNS ARE HALLELUJAHS

Great hymns are great poetry. Great poetry paints word pictures that capture our imagination. Sing or read the following hymns and let your "mind's eye" explore the imagery that is in each. Which are your favorite "word pictures?"

- Our God, Our Help in Ages Past (LW 180)
- Up Through Endless Ranks of Angels (LW 152)
- Jesus, Your Blood and Righteousness (LW 362)
- Rock of Ages (LW 361)
- O God, O Lord of Heaven and Earth (LW 319)
- Thy Strong Word Did Cleave the Darkness (LW 328)
- Amid the World's Bleak Wilderness (LW 273)

Compare and contrast the hymn "Salvation unto Us Has Come" (LW 355) with Jaroslav Vajda's paraphrase, "The Rescue We Were Waiting For."

THE RESCUE WE WERE WAITING FOR

The rescue we were waiting for
Has come most undeservedly,
While we were groping on the floor
Of deep despair, what did we see?
The hand of Jesus, God's own Son,
Came reaching down to us alone:
No one but he could save us.

Chained by the law and its demands
And crippled by the curse of sin,
All offerings smeared by guilty hands,
The walls of hopelessness closed in,
While in the mirror all I saw
Was weakling, rebel, fatal flaw —
And found no one to save me.

The law, I found, was not the way
To life and health, to joy and peace;
I'd piled up debts I could not pay,
From death there was no sure release.
And then, when in the deepest throes
Of gloom, I heard the hammer blows
Constructing my salvation.

The gift I had no right to claim,
A life to compensate my loss,
By grace from God the Father came:
My substitute upon my cross.
My pardon there was read to me,
Beneath that God-forsaken tree —
And I am free forever!

Secure within his warm embrace,
Join in the Savior's freedom song:
Show Christ to every downcast face,
Shout Christ to all the dying throng!
Sing loving Father, gracious Son,
Sing living Spirit, freedom won,
For now and through all ages!

THE IMAGERY OF THE PSALMS

The book of Psalms was the worship book—the hymnal—of the Old Testament believer. It is rich in the language of adoration, confession, thanksgiving, and supplication. Study the psalms below. Notice the pictures the psalmists paint with their words. Identify the psalm that best captures your imagination. Pick a psalm other than the ones listed below and help your class "see" its imagery by describing it to them.

46 _____

47 _____

113 _____

114 _____

130 _____

136 _____

GROWING IN WORSHIP

1. Here is an exercise to challenge your imagination. Read the story of David and Goliath in 1 Samuel 17. Then compare it to Martin Luther's hymn, A Mighty Fortress Is Our God. How does the hymn capture the message and emotion of the Bible passage?

_____

_____

_____

_____

_____

_____

2. Devise some creative ways of singing (or speaking) the five songs of the "ordinary" discussed earlier in this chapter. Perhaps a music teacher, choir director, or organist could give some advice.

INNOVATION

WORSH**I**P IS **I**NNOVATION

6

Worship is order, but with this order comes a built-in opportunity for changes and additions that provide for variety and keep our response to God fresh and contemporary. In this chapter we want to look at some of the innovations that can be included in the worship life of the congregation.

The weekly worship celebration, the **Divine Service**, contains variety because it follows a **two-fold pattern**: in the first part of the liturgy we concentrate on the **Word of God**, and in the second part the focus is on the celebration of the **Sacrament**. Within the service, there are certain parts—called "**the Ordinary**"—which remain unchanged from week to week, and other parts—called "**the Propers**"—which are different every Sunday.

THE ORDINARY

Invocation
Confession and Absolution
Kyrie
Hymn of Praise
Creed
Preface
Sanctus
Lord's Prayer
Words of Institution
Peace
Agnus Dei
Post-Communion Canticle
Post-Communion Prayer
Benediction

These **unchanging** parts of the service give stability, shape, and structure to our prayer life. They remind us of the tremendous scope of God's grace and teach us to come into his presence with the boldness and confidence that comes with being members of God's family—his redeemed sons and daughters—princes and princesses of heaven.

THE PROPERS

Collect
Scripture Readings
Gradual
Verse
Offertory
Prayer of the Church
Hymns

These **changing** parts of the service ensure that we hear and tell the "whole story" of our salvation over the course of a year. They provide "something new" for each Sunday.

Further variety is possible within the Divine Service because not all the parts of the liturgy have to be done every week. Look for the word *may* in the **rubrics** (the instructions printed in red). That little word indicates that the following part of the service is optional. We may also choose to add things to the service, or make certain parts more elaborate on special occasions.

Occasional Services

Throughout the history of the church, other services, such as the **Order of Matins** and the **Order of Vespers**, have been added to the church's liturgy to enrich her worship life. Liturgies have been designed for **baptisms, weddings, funerals**, and other special events in the church's life. These special services normally include **praise, proclamation**, and **prayer.**

Within these three general categories are included an invocation, general or specific prayers, the reading of Scripture, preaching, hymns, an offering, and a benediction. *Lutheran Worship* contains several special services on pages 199–312. Let's take a look at them.

Matins and Vespers

The orders for morning and evening worship have a long history in the life of the Christian church. In the Old Testament, sacrifices were to be made every day in the morning and in the evening (Exodus 29:38–46). The apostles kept some of the practices of the Jewish synagogue which included morning and evening services (Acts 3:1). The word **Matins** comes from the Latin word **matutinus**, which means **"belonging to the morn-**

ing." The word **Vespers** comes from the word **vespera,** meaning "**evening.**"

These services give God's people an opportunity to join together in worship using psalms, hymns, Scripture lessons, responses, prayers, and canticles. In these orders the worshiper adores, speaks, listens, and prays. These orders can also be used for meetings, family worship, and private devotions.

Morning and Evening Prayer

To mark the transition between light and darkness, Morning Prayer gives thanks for the rising of the sun in connection with Christ's resurrection. Evening Prayer gives attention to the setting of the sun and expresses thanks for Christ's light in the midst of darkness. These prayers are also suitable for small group devotions and can add great depth and richness to the family's prayer life.

Other Prayers

One of the oldest forms of prayer is **Compline** (page 263)—prayer before retiring. You might call this order the bedtime prayer of the church. The theme is one of trust in God as Protector and Provider.

The **Responsive** and **Bidding Prayers,** the **Litany,** and the **Daily Prayer Guides** and **Lectionary** (pages 270–299) are useful tools to help God's people grow and mature in their prayer life. They include petitions asking for God's mercy and deliverance, intercessions asking for God's help in time of need, and thanksgiving for God's continual blessings.

A fitting summary of this discussion on innovation is found in the Introduction to *Lutheran Worship:*

"We are heirs of an astonishingly rich tradition. Each generation receives from those who went before and, in making that tradition . . . its own, adds what best may serve its own day—the living heritage and something new"

When we are moved by the Holy Spirit to worship "in spirit and in truth" (John 4:24 NIV), we, too, stand in that long line of God's saints who have received with thanksgiving "the living heritage" and added their own "something new." The highest goal of worship is expressed in the closing lines of Martin Franzmann's hymn "O God, O Lord of Heaven and Earth" (*LW* 319):

"Each life a high doxology / Unto the Holy Trinity."

PERSONAL
BUT NOT PRIVATE

WORSHI**P** IS **P**ERSONAL
BUT NOT PRIVATE

7

In Baptism, God touches each of us individually; He calls us by name and makes us His own. In the Lord's Supper we individually receive the forgiveness of sins. Jesus says to each of us, "this is my body, which is given *for you* . . . this is my blood . . . which is shed *for you* for the forgiveness of sins." The Good News is that our relationship with God is very personal. We are His and He is ours.

But the Good News is also that we are not alone in our faith. God's touch in baptism brings us into the family of God; through baptism we are called into a community of God's people. We grow and are nurtured within that community throughout our lives, and our worship takes place in a community as well. We are individual members of the corporate body of Christ. Our relationship is always a personal one, but it is never private.

As a gifted member of the body of Christ, what special blessings, talents, abilities, or attitudes do you bring to the worship life of your congregation?

THE CHURCH YEAR

When we celebrate the special events of our lives—baptisms, birthdays, confirmation, graduation, anniversaries, funerals,—we naturally gather our family and our friends around us. In each of our lives there is a cycle of "gathering times" when we remember the events that are important to our family. These times are very personal, but they are not intended to be private. For example, I may speak of *my* birthday, but my birthday has brought me into a family, so we celebrate the event together. In the same way, I join other family members in celebrating their birthdays. My participation is important to them, just as their participation is important to me. Each year, as I join in this round of celebrations, my understanding and commitment to my family and friends grows.

The church year provides for the family of God a round of celebrations that helps us grow in our understanding and commitment to Jesus Christ and each other as members of His body, the church. Our regular celebrations happen on the Lord's day—Sunday—each week. Each Sunday is like a little Easter celebration, when we remember first of all the resurrection of Jesus Christ, that event which is central to our faith and life together.

Read what St. Paul says about this resurrection event and its implications for the church in 1 Corinthians 15, especially verses 12–28.

Our Sunday celebrations are grouped into seasons. **The church year is divided into two halves:**

The Festival Half

In the Festival Half of the church year we celebrate the events of Jesus' life through a cycle of preparation and celebration.

The Half Year of the Church

In the Half Year of the church year we reflect on the teachings of Jesus for the church and the meaning of discipleship through a longer time of study and growth. Some call this half the "green meadow" of faith development.

During this two-fold cycle of the church year, the whole story of our salvation is told, and we have time to mature and develop in our faith under the Word of God.

THE CHURCH YEAR

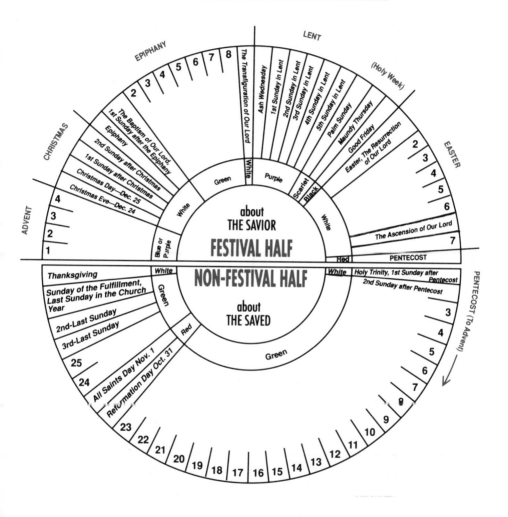

Note: More than 52 weeks are shown because there can be up to 28 Sundays after Pentecost, and up to 9 Sundays after the Epiphany, but never both in the same year. Some festivals also fall during the week.

THE CHURCH BUILDING

Throughout this study we have been reminding ourselves that we don't just "go to church," but that **we are the church**. However, if we worship faithfully, we will spend a considerable amount of time in church buildings over the course of our lives. Church buildings can say a lot about a community's understanding of worship. What are the most outstanding features of your church building? What would you change to make the building better reflect your growing understanding of worship?

What features of your church building encourage the PERSONAL aspects of worship?

What features of your church building encourage the COMMUNITY aspects of worship?

Let's consider three categories of church architecture.

Gothic

Gothic style architecture comes down to us from the Middle Ages. Churches built in this style are long and narrow. The many arches are designed to focus attention upward, on God, and to emphasize the communication between Him and us. Many Gothic churches have transepts on either side so that the building is in the shape of a cross. The choir and organ are often in the rear where they can best support and encourage the congregation's singing.

In-The-Round

This style of building emphasizes the community aspect of worship. We can see the faces of many other worshipers. The organist and the choir are not separated from the rest of the congregation. Baptism and the Lord's Supper are celebrated in the middle of the gathered assembly.

Theater-Style

The pastor, readers, and musicians are usually in front on a raised platform so that worshipers can see and hear more effectively. The seats are gradually higher toward the back, as in a theater. There is often little art or decoration. The church is designed to be practical and to seat as many people as efficiently as possible.

Discuss the positive and negative aspects of each of these architectural styles for worship. Which do you prefer? Why?

Visit other church buildings in your community and compare them to your own. What statements do the buildings make about what is important to the people who worship there?

The worship life of a Christian congregation is one of the main tools the Holy Spirit uses to shape and form us spiritually. God also uses our participation to help shape and form the spirituality of others. Our orders of worship, observance of the church year, fellowship with other believers, and building in which we meet all help us, under the guidance of the Holy Spirit, to be what God has declared us to be:

a community of believers,
the body of Christ, and
the family of God.

GROWING IN WORSHIP

1. Read and discuss what St. Paul says about the community of believers, the body of Christ, in 1 Corinthians 12:12–27 and Romans 12:4–13.

2. Read and discuss the construction of the tabernacle (Exodus 25–27, 30, 36–38, 40) and the temple (1 Kings 6–7). In what ways were they similar to our modern churches, and in what ways were they different? Why do you think God told His people in the Old Testament what buildings they were to build for worship, while in the New Testament God never tells us what sort of churches to build?

3. Look in a concordance and select any ten passages from the New Testament that use the word **church**. (The Old Testament uses the words *congregation* and *assembly* in place of the word *church*.) What do the New Testament writers mean by the term? Did people "go to church" or "attend church" as we do today? Is it true that the Christians *are* the church?

4. Choose a season of the church year and study the lessons for each Sunday in the season. What is most important about the season? Come up with some ideas for enhancing worship in your congregation during that season.

APPENDIX 1

SOME COMMON WORDS AND PHRASES USED IN WORSHIP

Absolution
The pronouncement of pardon or forgiveness of sins.

Acolyte
One who serves in the chancel; lights and extinguishes the candles.

Agnus Dei
Latin for **Lamb of God.**

Alleluia
An Old Testament Hebrew word meaning **"Praise Yahweh"** or "Praise the LORD." (Yahweh is the Hebrew proper name of God and is usually translated "the LORD.")

Amen
An Old Testament Hebrew word meaning **"so be it; it is true."**

Apostles' Creed
A confession of faith in the Triune God formulated by the early Christian church. It is faithful to the teaching of the apostles.

Baptistry
The place where the baptismal font is located.

Breaking of Bread
An early name for the Lord's Supper (Acts 2:42; 20:7).

Canticle
A liturgical text based on scripture, usually sung.

Celebrant
The pastor who leads the celebration of the Lord's Supper.

Choir
A group of singers who help lead the congregation in worship.

Collect
A brief prayer.

Communion
Sharing something or having something in common; often used as a name for the Lord's Supper (1 Corinthians 10:16, where NIV translates *communion* as **"participation"**).

Confession
(1) An admission of sins, either in a public service or in private to a pastor or another person; (2) a statement of Christian faith and belief.

Consecrate	To declare holy, dedicate to God; often used of speaking the Words of Institution over the bread and wine in the celebration of the Lord's Supper.
Crucifix	A cross with the body of Christ on it. The crucifix emphasizes the incarnation of Christ and His sacrifice for our sins.
Devotion	A brief worship service.
Disciple	A follower of Jesus Christ.
Distribution	Serving the Lord's Supper.
Doctrine	A religious teaching or belief.
Doxology	Praise to God, usually naming the three persons of the Trinity.
Ecclesia (ek-lay-SEE-ah)	The usual New Testament Greek word for the **church,** the body of believers in Christ.
Elohim (el-o-HEEM)	The most common Old Testament Hebrew word for **God.** A shortened form is El (ale), as in Emmanu-EL.
Emmanuel	Hebrew name meaning **"with us (is) God"** (Isaiah 7:14; 8:8, 10); applied to Christ in Matthew 1:23.
Epistle	A **letter;** New Testament epistles are letters sent by the apostles to churches. (For example, Romans is the letter St. Paul sent to the church at Rome.) Worship services usually include an Epistle Lesson.
Eucharist	A Greek word meaning **"giving thanks."** It is another name for the Lord's Supper because Jesus "gave thanks" over the bread and wine in the Last Supper.
Evensong	Evening worship, sometimes called the Order of Vespers.
Ewer	A pitcher for pouring water into the baptismal font.
Feast Day	A major church celebration such as Christmas or Easter.
Font	The vessel that holds the water used for baptism (related to the word *fountain*.)

Gloria Patri	Latin for **"glory to the Father."** It is the name of a hymn of praise to the Father, Son, and Holy Spirit.
Gloria in Excelsis	A Latin phrase meaning **"glory in the highest [place], glory to God in heaven"** (Psalm 148:1; Luke 2:14). It is a hymn of adoration and praise to the Trinity.
Holy Week	The week between Palm Sunday and Easter Sunday.
Homily	A short, informal sermon based on a Biblical text or theme.
Host	(1) Term for unleavened bread used in the Lord's Supper. (2) Word for angels, "the heavenly host"; also used for the armies of Israel. "Lord of Sabaoth," meaning "Lord of hosts," probably refers to God as Lord over both angels in heaven and armies on earth.
Hosanna	Hebrew word meaning **"Save now, we pray"** (Psalm118:25). Used as a shout of praise for Christ (Matthew 21:9).
Hymn	A song of prayer, praise, adoration, or thanksgiving to God.
Individual Cup	Small cups used for distributing the blood of Christ to each communicant in the Lord's Supper; often used instead of the one common cup.
Introit	Latin word meaning **"he enters."** It is a psalm sung or spoken at the beginning of the service.
Invitatory	A Latin word meaning **"invitation."** It is an opening sentence in the liturgy for the Order of Matins.
Kyrie	Greek word meaning **"O Lord."** It is a responsive chant following the Introit in Divine Service II.
Lectionary	A book of Scripture readings for the church year.
Litany	Greek word meaning **"prayer,"** referring to responsive prayers spoken by pastor and people.

Liturgy	Greek word meaning **"service."** It is the order of worship followed by the congregation.
Liturgical Color	The colors used in the church according to the season of the church year. The colors are white, black, red, violet, blue, green, scarlet, and gold. See page 8 of *Lutheran Worship*.
Lord's Supper	One of the oldest names for the Sacrament which Jesus instituted at His Last Supper (1 Corinthians 11:20). It is also called Holy Communion.
Magnificat	Latin word meaning **"magnify, praise."** The first word of the song of Mary (Luke 1:46–55), sung as the canticle at the services of Evening Prayer and Vespers.
Maundy Thursday	The Thursday in Holy Week when the Lord's Supper was instituted. **"Maundy"** is Latin for **"command,"** referring to Jesus' "new commandment of love" (John 13:34).
Minor Services	The worship service orders other than the main service of Holy Communion, such as Matins, Vespers, Morning Prayer, the litany, the suffrages, etc.
Nicene Creed	The statement of faith adopted by the Council of Nicaea (A. D. 325), confessed in the service when the Lord's Supper is celebrated.
Nunc Dimittis	Latin for meaning **"now let you servant depart"** based on Simeon's song (Luke 2:29–32); may be sung after the distribution of Holy Communion or as the canticle at Vespers.
Offertory	Music sung when the offering is received and presented at the altar.
Ordinary	The parts of the service that are the same every week.
Pall	The cloth used to cover the coffin at a funeral.
Paraments	The cloth decorations in the chancel on the altar, pulpit, lectern, etc. The paraments are changed to match the color for the season of the church year.

Pax Domini	Latin for **"the peace of the Lord."**
Propers	The parts of the service that change each week, such as the Scripture readings, the Introit, the Gradual, etc.
Preface	The part of the liturgy leading to the celebration of the Lord's Supper. There is a preface for each season of the church year (*Lutheran Worship* pages 145–148).
Responsory	Scripture verses sung or spoken after the reading of a lesson.
Rite	A Christian ceremony such as a wedding, funeral, confirmation, installation, etc., which is not a sacrament.
Ritual	A procedure or set of actions done as part of a religious ceremony. Christian rituals may include kneeling, making the sign of the cross, etc.
Rubrics	The rules that govern the order of a liturgical service. The word comes from Latin for **"red,"** and the rubrics are in red in *Lutheran Worship*.
Sacraments	Sacraments combine the Word of God with an earthly element (water, bread, wine). Jesus told us to perform two sacraments; Holy Baptism and the Lord's Supper (Matthew 28:19; Luke 22:19). By the power of the Holy Spirit, God bestows grace, the forgiveness of sins, and eternal life through them.
Salutation	A greeting between pastor and people.
Sanctus	A song of praise that concludes the Preface in the Holy Communion liturgy. It is based on Isaiah 6:3 and Matthew 21:9.
Stanza	A verse of a hymn.
Suffrage	A responsive prayer.
Versicles	Short Scripture verses or sentences that call the congregation to worship and reflect the theme for the day.
Vestments	The special garments worn by the pastor, acolytes, choir, and others who help lead the worship service.

APPENDIX 2

CHURCH BUILDING TERMS

Altar

Usually made of marble or wood, it is located in the center of the chancel. Since sacrifices in the Old Testament were made on an altar, it reminds us of the sacrifice of Jesus Christ for us. It also serves as the **"table"** for the Lord's Supper. The altar is the holiest place of God's presence in the church building and the focus of much of the service.

Chancel

The front part of the church where the pastor stands during the service. It is often raised slightly. The altar, pulpit, lectern, and communion rail are all in the chancel.

Gallery

The area for the choir and the organ. In Gothic-style churches this is often a balcony in the back of the church.

Lectern

The stand from which the lessons are read.

Narthex

The room or hall at the entrance of the church building.

Nave

The main part of the church where the congregation is seated during worship. Comes from Latin for **"ship."**

Prie-Dieu

A small desk for kneeling and prayer in the chancel. French, meaning **"pray to God."**

Pulpit

The place where the pastor preaches the sermon. It usually is raised and enclosed on three sides.

Sacristy

A small room, usually with a door to the chancel, where the elements are prepared for the sacraments. The vessels, paraments, and candles are often kept there.

Sanctuary Lamp	A candle or light, kept burning continually, which represents the presence of Christ, who is the Light of the world.
Sedilia	The seats in the chancel for the pastor and acolytes.
Vestry	A small room, usually with a door to the chancel, for storing the vestments and for the pastor to prepare for worship. Sometimes one room is used as both the sacristy and the vestry.

APPENDIX 3

VESSELS USED FOR HOLY COMMUNION

Chalice   A large cup used to administer the wine.

Ciborium   A cup-like vessel in which the wafers are kept.

Corporal   A square white linen placed on the altar, on which the vessels for the Lord's Supper are set.

Flagon   A pitcher containing the wine to be poured into the chalice.

Paten   A plate used to carry the wafers.

Veil   A cloth placed over the vessels while they are on the altar.

Ciborium   Chalice   Flagon

Paten   Silk veil

67

APPENDIX 4

Altar Terms

Dorsal

A curtain on the wall behind the altar used when there is no reredos.

Fair Linen

Cloth of fine linen covering the entire top of the altar.

Mensa

The flat top of the altar.

Missal Stand

A small book stand placed on the mensa to hold the worship book.

Reredos

A large framework of wood or stone behind and above the altar in some churches.

Retable

A small shelf rising above the rear of the mensa. Candles are usually placed on the retable.

Throne

A shelf built into the center of the retable to hold the cross.